DEVON REFLECTIONS

Jilly Carter

BOSSINEY BOOKS

First published in 1990 by
Bossiney Books, St. Teath, Bodmin, Cornwall.

Typeset and printed by Penwell Limited,
Callington, Cornwall.

ISBN 0 948158 65 4

ACKNOWLEDGEMENTS

Front cover photography: Courtesy of Ilfracombe Museum.
Back cover photography: R.E. Jones.
Other photographs: Ralph Alford; John Bower; Cookworthy Museum;
Judy Diss; Mr Hockaday; Ilfracombe Museum; R.E. Jones; G.L. Moon;
Okehampton Museum; Les Retallick; Philip Stone; TSW; Jack Tuze;
Hilary Wreford; Alf Worth.

JILLY CARTER, well-known on regional and national television, follows her highly acclaimed **Cornish Reflections** with this new book about Devon in the old days.

Born at Widnes, Cheshire, in 1953 and educated near Liverpool, she acquired a BA London degree in English, French and History of Art. She then went to Paris, teaching and modelling Spring collections for various Paris fashion houses. Later she moved to Lisbon for more teaching – and later to Rome. In Rome she did more teaching, helped to research an historical travel book on Darius the Great, read the news on an American radio station and presented the Girl Friday Show.

Jilly Carter came back to do Radio 4 presentation, before moving to Bournemouth where she became a disc jockey presenter on a live daily show. It was television that brought her to the Westcountry, when in 1982 she joined Television South West. She began at Plymouth working with Gus Honeybun as a continuity announcer and was then promoted to the Newsroom as a presenter and reporter on the nightly 'Today' programme. Since then she has worked on a variety of programmes including 'The Business Show'. She also had the distinction of presenting live satellites with a station in North Carolina to celebrate their 400th anniversary.

Jilly left TSW in May 1989. Recently she has worked as a freelance journalist and presenter for both BBC and ITN in London – and she presents live satellite broadcasts in Europe for international companies.

In 1988 she made her debut for Bossiney with **Cornish Reflections.** Now comes its natural successor – **Devon Reflections.** It is a nostalgic journey but Jilly's thoughtful text and the rich harvest of old photographs underline the paradox of those far-off days: 'Life wasn't all tranquil leafy lanes and charming thatched cottages . . . life, for many, was tough.'

In her years with Television South West, Jilly Carter travelled thousands of miles for news stories and interviews; she now uses that knowledge – and affection for Devon – in producing a balanced polished portrait of the county. Words and pictures make this book a must for all who care for Devon and her glorious past.

Nothing is now known of this large Victorian family of farmers from the Torquay area, but they make a marvellous study. All virtues are here; sobriety, self-discipline, diligence, hard work and steadfastness. Let's hope they also managed to have some fun in their spare time.

'A COUNTY which is all but the largest in the kingdom; which has afforded the earliest traces of the existence of man in these islands; which has never from the dawn of recorded history occupied a second place in the national life, whose worthies, century by century, claim the first rank in every class – soldiers, statesmen, poets, inventors, men of science – the history of such a county is the history of England' – a glowing description of Devon, in a nineteenth century travel guide. But the author, although waxing a trifle lyrical, has made an accurate summary of the importance of Devon in the nation's development.

From the earliest traces of Palaeolithic man, the Celts, the Saxons, the Romans, to the arrival of William the Conqueror,

The picturesque village of East Ogwell, near Newton Abbot, at hay-making time. The thatched cottages still stand, and the village hall is on the left.

The siren's sounded, and there's no hanging around for this group of factory workers from Heathcote's Mill at Tiverton. The factory, which still exists today, was famous for its machine-made lace, and belonged to the famous Nottingham industrialist John Heathcote. Originally the factory began in that city, but was moved to Tiverton in 1816. This photo is dated around 1910, and captures young and old in jolly mood off to lunch.

Devon has been a county to be reckoned with. Its heyday came in the reign of Elizabeth I, when Devon produced such great men as Raleigh, Drake, Hawkins, Grenville and Gilbert. She was never a county out of the news; in the 1688 Revolution, William III chose Brixham as his landing place. Plymouth was the first borough to declare for him; Newton Abbot proclaimed him king, and Exeter gave him troops and support. Devon's reputation for building boats and breeding fighting men went before her, so she was heavily relied upon to help win the war against Napoleon and the French, and she played her part in defeating the Germans in two World Wars.

What other county can easily match Devon's track record in producing some of the greatest seamen, navigators and seafighters, of soldiers like Monk and Marlborough, of painters such as Hudson and Reynolds, of bishops such as Henry Phillpots and Frederick Temple? Not to mention rather more notorious characters, like the pirate Robert Nutt, the scourge of the Channel, or Thomas Benson, the MP for Bideford, who defied the government of George III by setting up a convict colony on Lundy Island and building up a thriving smuggling trade. Or the parson's son from Bickleigh, a certain Bampfylde Moore-Carew, who became known as the King of the Gypsies. An expert dissembler, he squeezed money out of the innocent by playing a variety of down-and-outs, ranging from a tin miner to a clergyman, a Greek refugee to a grandmother of three!

Sir Walter Raleigh described Devon as the county of red earth, ruddy apples, rosy cheeks and honest men. It has nine thousand miles of roads and two coastlines. It's probably Britain's most popular tourist area, and millions of people can't be wrong. They come for its glorious beaches – the ones that still aren't too polluted – its rolling valleys, the variety of landscape offered by the Moors, the marshes, the estuaries, the heathland. They marvel at the narrow winding lanes, revealing tiny villages full of thatched cob cottages, and the vast hedgerows, bursting with primroses and daffodils, many of which were planted during the two Wars, when land was at a premium and gardens were a luxury. They probably also bemoan the fact that Devon seems to have more than its fair share of rainfall, and would have wholeheartedly agreed with the poet John Keats, who was quite ascerbic about Devon's attractions in the rain: 'You may say what you will of Devonshire; the truth is that it is a splashy, rainy, misty, snowy, foggy, haily, floody, muddy, slipshod county . . . the flowers here wait as naturally for rain twice a day as mussels do for the tide'.

But rainy weather can be an opportunity to discover Devon's other face, the other side of the chocolate-box image of thatched cottages and clotted cream teas. That's when the dark and brooding nature of the county appears, in places like Dartmoor, with its granite outcrops making a superb backdrop to a roman-

A beach scene at Exmouth, described in the early nineteenth century by a doctor thus; ... 'but for an occasional sea fog after the heat of a summer's day, Exmouth is free from mist and damp vapours, and in common with Budleigh Salterton, is less likely to rain than in other places in the neighbourhood, ... a resort for weakly children and those of a scrofulous constitution has shown often to be greatly benefitted'. No self-respecting Victorian, as pre-occupied as he often was with his health, would ignore such good medical advice! Also, Exmouth was the perfect place for taking steamer trips to Teignmouth, Torquay and Dartmouth.

7

Travelling by pony and trap must have been thirsty business on dry, dusty roads, so what better place to stop for refreshment than a country pub. Here a group of travellers dismount from a small wagonette outside the Cat and Fiddle at Sowton, on the Sidmouth road. They'd probably ridden from Exeter. The ladies would partake of a glass in the garden at the back, while the gentlemen would retire to prop up the bar.

tic, but bleak and eerie landscape. For those who wish to delve deeper, the mystical nature of Devon waits to be discovered. Thankfully there is still the space in Devon to absorb all the enthusiastic visitors, and space for those who wish to lose themselves in the natural beauty of this very special place.

There really must be something in the Devon air that encourages and inspires talent, for Devon has certainly produced its fair share of creative people. Literary lights include Henry Williamson, Dame Agatha Christie, Sabine Baring-Gould. And there's William Browne, the poet of Tavistock, and the celebrated Samuel Taylor Coleridge, who was born at Ottery St Mary. In the world of art, Plympton proudly hails its famous son Joshua Reynolds, who painted more than two thousand stunning pictures which continue to bring joy to generation after generation. Painting on a smaller scale came from the miniaturist Richard Cosway of Tiverton. And nobody can remain indifferent to the work of the highly controversial and colourful Robert Lenkiewicz, whose murals adorn many a wall in the historic city of Plymouth.

The Palmer family, outside Bratton Clovelly Post Office. The two grandmothers, dressed in black, look suitably proud of their offspring. The village boasts one of the best – and least-known – churches in Devon, dating from the fourteenth century. The parish had many farm houses with Celtic names, such as Maindea and Breazle. Bratton gets its second name from the Clavilles, who held the manor in the thirteenth century.

Old Central Station Queen Street, in Exeter, in the summer of 1904, and the first Chagford omnibus stands, waiting for passengers. The London South West Railway service began in this year, but it was to be short-lived, for the Milner Daimler 16-horse power bus hadn't reckoned with Devon's steep hills, so the service ran for one season only. It was replaced by a fifty horse-power model, which continued to run the route until 1924, and was a rival of the Great West Railway service.

Not only has the county inspired sailors like Sir Francis Drake, and the more contemporary Sir Francis Chichester, but explorers on land too. Captain Robert Falcon Scott may have failed in his attempt to be first at the South Pole, but he has earned a place in history as the man who followed his dream, to the farthest outposts of the earth.

But we must not – and do not – forget the women who have made their mark on this county; the formidable character of Lady Nancy Astor, who Plymouth will never forget. A striking, indomitable person, who was a symbol of courage and determination during the war years, and whose example many women tried to emulate. She gave them the conviction that women did have a rightful place in Parliament, and MPs such as Dame Janet Fookes and Emma Nicholson, both of who have constituencies here, are just two who've followed in her footsteps. I have a personal debt of gratitude to Lady Astor; she opened the Margaret McMillan Nursery School on Plymouth's Hoe, where my daughter Lizzie has spent two very happy years.

Outside Westminster, women like Lady Sylvia Sayer fight what must seem like a lone battle at times, to protect the precarious balance of nature on Dartmoor, and Ruth Murray has done her

Twenty-six young maids-a-milking, or hoping to, if they complete their training at the Devon County Dairy School. Classes were from nine to twelve, and two to five, and visitors were encouraged to come round, at a cost of 3d. The girls sit, composed, in spotless pinafores, hair in chignons, all portraying noble Victorian virtues of cleanliness and seriousness.

bit to safeguard the wildlife of the Moor by opening her own badger sanctuary.

When I was a reporter for Television South West, I travelled thosuands of miles over Devon and Cornwall. In my first book, *Cornish Reflections,* I was privileged to meet many special people who invited me into their homes, and who shared with me their memories of what the county was like at the turn of the century, and how it has changed. Through their precious photographs, I traced a journey back in time, to a more leisurely existence, when people had time to exchange the odd word, to enquire about their neighbours, to be aware of, and be in harmony with, the natural world around them. In this, my second book, I have tried to capture a similar flavour of the beautiful county of Devon, as she was over a hundred years ago.

It's easy to become sentimental when pouring over old photographs, and the temptation to indulge in nostalgia is very strong. Life wasn't all tranquil leafy lanes and charming thatched cottages for the locals. Life, for many, was tough; eking out an existence in an often bleak environment was all that concerned many. But, as in Cornwall over a hundred years ago, there was much to be said for the rural life, for the isolation and peace of the countryside, far away from the grimmer industrial cities to the north and east. As Raleigh said, people were honest and straightforward, and they respected the land and sea on which they depended for their livelihood. I hope that the photographs I have chosen in this book capture something of what has passed away, but not been forgotten, and that those who look at them will enjoy reflecting on them as much as I have.

Perhaps the last word should go to the writer Arthur Mee, who mused 'what do they know of England who do not know DEVON?'

North Street, Exeter, about 1890, and the heat is on. Sunblinds are dropped to keep off the flies and lower the temperature, giving a ramshackle, rather shabby aspect to the narrow street. In the distance, the cast iron bridge put up in 1830 spanning Longbrook, which ran down into the Exe, and made its steep northern approach so attractive to the Romans centuries before.

13

Exeter

Mr W.A. Milton, the well-known Exeter photographer, caused quite a curious crowd to gather when he brought his apparatus to Preston Street, Exeter in 1895. Poor folk weren't used to having their photos taken, and curtains twitched as he arrived. Mr Milton may have been more interested in the architecture of Preston Street, which is first mentioned in 1160. Close by is Rack Street which took its name from the racks which were put out to dry the city's cloth. Note the drain down the middle of Preston Street.

A beautifully-executed photograph of the corner of High Street and North Street, Exeter. Standing guard is the carved wooden figure of St Peter, which in ancient times probably supported the dragon post, and stood at ground level. When the chemists' shop was rebuilt, about 1897, this statue was re-erected on the new Hapworth shop, and apart from the war years, it remained there until the 1980s. The figures in the photo are composed, almost as if photography were becoming old hat; the girl with hand on hip, the man casually leaning against a shop front.

*Water Lane and Leat Terrace,
looking west, with St Mary's Steps
church in the background. The
leat was used in the process of
fulling cloth, which was
flattened and hammered by
water-driven equipment, to
achieve the right texture. This
photograph was taken around
1914 by A.W. Searley, an
inspector of schools.*

The Exeter Quay ferry, which dates back to medieval times. Originally the ferry carried passengers to the St Thomas side of the city, but here it's taking people across to the canal basin. The ferry still runs in summer as a service for the Maritime Museum.

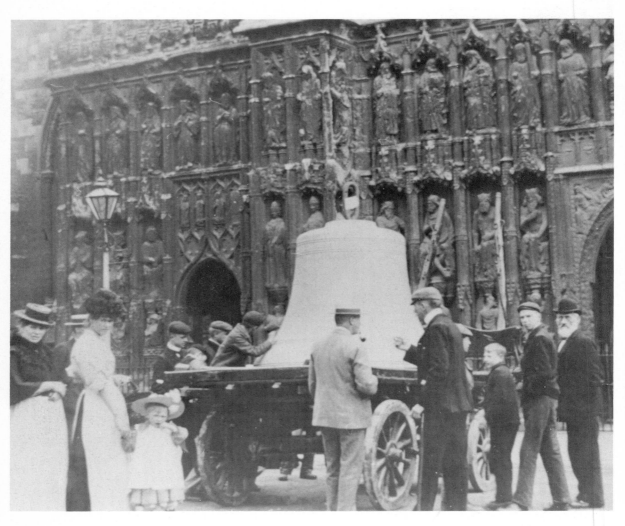

A fascinating photograph of the west front of Exeter Cathedral, as a crowd of locals comes to inspect the Fox Bell, one of two which were re-hung around 1902. The other was called Grandison, but careful scrutiny of the Latin inscription on this one verifies it is Fox that's causing the stir here. A be-capped school lad is about to tap it with his fist to check the resonance is OK!

Exeter's famous Stepcote Hill, part of the west quarter which was cleared when the city began to get rid of its slums in the 1930s. The houses, built in the sixteenth century, must have been very dark inside, which probably accounts for the fact that most people spent much of their time outdoors, sitting on the cobblestones or standing around exchanging gossip. Not a very fertile place for a small child's imagination, though. This particular house escaped the bulldozers, and until recently was a jeweller's shop.

EXETER High Street, looking west of Eastgate. the GPO, built in 1884, is on the left, and replaced the Grammar School, which occupied the monastic buildings of St John. On the right, the statue of Henry VII above Markrow Furnishers. Henry VII had a particular significance for Exeter. The city remained loyal to the Crown during the Prayerbook revolution, so the king gave it the status of a city and a county, with its own assizes. This meant the sheriff of Devon had no jurisdiction inside Exeter. Here in this photograph, it's eleven in the morning, 1897, and the High Street is busy with traffic and people going about their daily lives. Shops have pegged out their sunshades on the pavement. Oh, that it were so easy to get round Exeter today!

The West Quarter – one of Exeter's poorest districts in the nineteenth century. Here, young children could be sure of a square meal for the price of just a farthing. The farthing breakfasts were begun by a charity which continued up until the 1930s, and its activities included day trips for children who'd never seen the countryside. From 1907 to 1908, the breakfasts were distributed for 71 days, providing 17,131 meals at a cost of £97. The cost of daily help to distribute the breakfasts totalled £18.5s 10d.

A marvellous view of traders at work in Exeter's High Street, dated 1874. We can be fairly sure of the year, because the first gabled house on the left was Huggins', a chemist's, which was built in front of All Hallows Church, and removed in 1879. On the left also, a knifegrinder, dressed in a black top hat, sharpens instruments while sitting at his cart. Small boys stand around; no school for them, it seems. They probably had full-time jobs, just like their elders.

Along the Exe

Ernest Alford, at Nether Exe, in front of one of the farm wagons. He worked on the farm from the age of 16 until he died in 1978. Drivers in those times had no reins on the horses, so they had to engage in a strange conversation with the horse, resulting in a particular kind of language:
Turn right – waing off
Turn left – come 'ere
Turn round – come 'ere back
Ernest knew all his shire horses well, and they never misunderstood him! The photo was taken around 1880, and Nether Exe Barton House is in the background.

Harvest time, and a family snack, or 'drinkins', in Nether Exe parish, with the Devon corn stitches, or stookes, in the background. Ernest Alford, a younger man here, relaxes with his young family, assisted by the maid Lily Mardon, who's serving up tea. Rover and Jack, the two dogs, are very much part of the family. Lily's grandmother was supposed to have been a white witch, and swears she heard Squire Young with his four-in-hand (four ponies pulling his carriage) riding through the village. He'd died several years before, and is buried in the churchyard. Stories apart, such refreshing picnic interludes were much welcomed in harvest-time, when workers toiled till well after eight o'clock on most nights.

A busy day's threshing at Nether Exe farm. In 1840, a certain Mr Christopher Hill from the parish went to make his fortune in London in the wine and spirit business. He returned home and bought Nether Exe, making it one of the most productive farms in Devon. It was blessed with good quality, flat arable land, and was famous for its old red Devon cattle. Here, George Shaw, of Broadclyst, near Exeter, has brought his threshing tackle, ably helped by his driver George Venn. Mr Venn had to walk from Broadclyst, with his mate, four miles across Killerton Park, to get up steam in the engine. Then he'd put in a day's work and have to walk all the way home. The equipment was kept at Frogmore, and had to be carted up and down narrow country lanes, wherever work was to be found. An enormous amount of tackle was needed to do the job. The steam engine would pull the big thresher and trusser, which tied the straw into sheaves. It was a job normally done well after harvest, more often in the New Year.

A chocolate-box-style idyllic country scene, down on the farm at Fernworthy, on Dartmoor. All the windows are thrown open, in this photograph taken by Frith in 1907, and two farm hands stop to chat in the shade, while a slouching lad peers at the camera. The farm probably belonged to the Mortemore family, and was re-built in 1690 in granite, using a rough stucco made of tallow, to protect it from the savage moorland winds and rain. The farm was on the edge of the famous Fernworthy Reservoir, and was given up on afforestation in 1917.

A pensive young lad in the village square at Lustleigh, in the Wray Valley. Its impressive moorland scenery was a magnet to visitors to Dartmoor, for they could look around the village, then move on to Lustleigh Cleave and Becky Falls nearby. Not far from the village station there's a block of granite, which probably formed part of an ancient Celtic cross. Legend has it that Bishop Grandisson dined off it, so it was renamed the Bishop's Stone.

Mother and children at Beardown, near Two Bridges. The boy is shoe-less, but the youngest looks fit and clean in her white pinafore. One hopes this tiny hovel was just used in summer, and that better accommodation was provided against the harsh Dartmoor winter.

A hardened bunch of miners, outside Ramsleigh Copper Mine, between Whiddon Down and Throwleigh. Round their necks they carry spare candles, which were often their only illumination underground. The candle was stuck to their helmet with a lump of hot wax. The mine was quite productive in its time and also included Wheal Emily. It was opened in 1850 and worked till 1880, was shut down for a while then continued until 1909. In 1902 the mine produced a hundred tons of copper ore a month. A steam engine provided the power for getting the tubs of ore on to the surface, and driving the pump to get rid of underground water. The ore was taken in trolleys on a tramway, to be crushed and sorted. A great deal of money was invested in expensive machinery, which proved not to be as effective as had been hoped. Falling prices, due to foreign imports, added to the mine's problems, so it was closed for good. During its last few years, it produced 3,752 tons of copper.

TWO VIEWS of the forbidding exterior of Princetown Prison on Dartmoor, the first dated 1890, with prisoners carrying tools for a day's hard labour, the other from 1905, with anxious women and children waiting to see their relatives. One thousand four hundred feet above sea level – the authorities couldn't have chosen a better spot in terms of bleakness and desolation. Dartmoor as a whole began to be opened up when a turnpike road was made in 1772. Large areas of moorland were taken over by 'improvers', one of them Thomas Tyrwhitt, who named Princetown after the Prince of Wales, later George IV. In 1805, Tyrwhitt was made Lord Warden of the Stannaries, and he became more and more involved with Dartmoor. During this time, England was at war with France, and many captured prisoners were shipped over to Millbay Prison. This soon became too small to cope with the ever-increasing numbers, so Tyrwhitt, now Sir Thomas Tyrwhitt, suggested a new prison should be built on his beloved Dartmoor. It was constructed of grey granite quarried from Herne Hole, and the foundation stone was laid in March 1806. The buildings, five to begin with, and later increased to seven, were designed like spokes in a wheel, within two circular walls. Escape was virtually impossible, and if it did occur, there were plenty of people with eyes peeled for runaways. Rewards for returning prisoners were high.

Firing practice on Okehampton range. Batteries of artillery used the ranges on the Moor for firing practice during the summer months, and long rows of sheds were erected as shelter for the horses. Most manoeuvres took place at Halstock Down. Wooden dummies were placed in rows to represent lines of soldiers, and a red flag was put up on Yes Tor and Watchet Hill one hour before practice commenced. It was intensely annoying during the tourist season when visitors wanted to roam freely, and dangerous for others; one Richard Hodge from Pudhanger was killed by a shell in 1880 while going about his daily business.

A charming postcard of a well-dressed little girl and her young brother out for the day at Simmons Park in Okehampton. The Park was a gift to the town in 1907 by Sydney Simmons, and adjoins the East Okement.

Another study in peaceful contemplation, as a lady, well-prepared for hiking with her stout boots, umbrella and hold-all, pauses for a brief rest at Aish Ridge, looking north towards Shipley. It's one of John Stabb's many Dartmoor scenes, always refreshing and charming to contemplate. The little dog, her companion, looks just the sort of dog to take on such a walk; sturdy, keen and frisky.

A marvellously evocative photograph from John Stabb, of a solitary Victorian lady lost in thought, as she surveys the landscape at Lustleigh Cleave, looking towards Manaton. For centuries, visitors like her have stood and paused, taking in the spectacular scenery and immense power of the natural world around us. Some things do not change, and this photo serves to remind us, and comfort us, of that fact.

Bovey Tracey, Coach starting for the Moors.

ALL SET for the off outside the Dolphin Hotel in Bovey Tracey, built in the late nineteenth century as a coaching house. The owner's name, John Joll, is proudly displayed over the porch. Horse-drawn wagonettes used to leave from here for trips to Dartmoor, to Becky Falls and to Widecombe. Bovey Tracey was much loved by the Victorians. It's situated at the basin of a lake filled by disintegrated granite from the Moor, and was renowned for its marsh plants. Beatrix Cresswell, in her handbook on Dartmoor in the latter part of the century, writes – 'it is a merry sight on a summer morning to see the coaches start from The Dolphin, and the sense of exhilaration is increased if we are to be among the passengers, for however fond we are of walking or cycling, I think every Briton feels a satisfaction of finding himself behind a good team.' Packed lunches of buns, biscuits and sandwiches, to be washed down with ale or lemonade, were provided, and the horses, Miss Cresswell notes, were not neglected either; 'One is glad to know that as soon as they get in, they have a mash with a bottle of gin in it; the drivers at The Dolphin have tried many pick-me-ups for the team after tremendous effort, finding gin the best of all.' The horses were not available for comment!

Torquay and

A leisurely promenade around Waldon Hill, on the west side of the harbour at Torquay. Before Torbay road was built, the cliffs of Waldon were continuously washed by the tides, and were subject to landslides. The rough and isolated summit of Waldon Hill was used to breed rabbits. It was later purchased by the Cary family, who went on to build the houses on Babbacombe Downs

Torquay, from Waldon Hill. F & Co.

*Palace Avenue, Paignton, around 1910. At the time, it was referred
to as 'withy-platters', for large numbers of willows and withies grew
there, and were an excellent source of raw material for basket makers
to construct their crabbing pots from. In fact it was a mecca for
natural products; young girls gathered camomile leaves for tea and
wine, and young boys collected leeches for local doctors. Most of
Paignton's flat lands were marshy swamps until they were reclaimed
in the nineteenth century, and Palace Avenue used frequently to be
under water.*

*Traffic brought to a standstill outside the Pavilion Theatre, Torquay,
which was opened in 1912. Crowds have thronged to welcome a
procession of World War I convalescing soldiers, who drive along in
open-top cars. And as they wend their way through the mêlée, the
band strikes up a tune. The men must have been very moved to see
such a welcome, with well-wishers pressing forward to cheer them on.
Architecturally, the public loos to the left, along with the fish and
coaling sheds, have long since gone. Behind we can see the new
marina. The Pavilion flourished as a theatre for many years, and
when there were moves to pull it down in the 1970s, members of
'Friends of the Pavilion' threatened to lie in front of the bulldozers to
stop such an act of sacrilege. Happily they won the day.*

Ah, men really were men in those days! A fine collection of knock-kneed gents assemble in the shivering cold of a Torquay winter, around 1910, before they take the plunge into the icy waters below. Not a wimp in sight.

A family group at Torquay. Mother hitches up her voluminous skirts to reveal lace petticoats, father rolls up his trousers, and the five offspring stare resolutely ahead into the camera lens. It all looks rather chilly and windswept. A group of passengers in a small boat look on in the distance. The picture was probably cherished as a memento of a good holiday.

GROWN WITH
HADFIELD'S
CHEMICAL
GUANO
BY
MR. A. E. MAUNDER

Mr. A. E. Maunder, Tavistowe Farm, Paignton, Devon, writes :—" This splendid Crop of Wheat was grown with your Chemical Guano which I can thoroughly recommend for all Crops."

One wonders how much Mr Maunder, of Tavistowe Farm, Paignton, was paid to advertise guano fertilizer, but he seems to do the job with conviction and due seriousness!

Tent life at Paignton. 263.

Down on the beach at Paignton in 1918 a family relaxes over afternoon tea, while nanny and the hound dog stand guard. In the background, the beach pier. A Victorian entrepreneur, Mr Arthur Hyde Dendy, bought Teignmouth Pier with the intention of bringing it to Paignton. But he had great problems dismantling it and re-assembling it in the town, so he abandoned the project and put up another in 1878. It was 750 feet long and had a grand pavilion at the end. Mr Hyde Dendy was a staunch supporter of Paignton, and was fiercely protective of the town when others compared it less favourably to neighbouring Torquay.

The Haldon Harriers, around 1905, gather for the hunt at Cockington, as a group of onlookers disdainfully try not to notice the hound cocking his leg. At least his sense of humour didn't desert him!

Plymouth

(GEORGE STREET PLYMOUTH & ELECTRIC TRAM-CAR.)

A busy George Street, Plymouth around 1910. The city had always been forward-thinking in terms of transport, and in 1880 the Plymouth, Devonport and District Tramways Company was set up. This company ran a single line from Millbay Street, via George Street, Lockyer Street and Princess Square, ending up at Hyde Park. It used five locomotives, hauling open-top cars, but it had a reputation for noisiness, unpunctuality and smoke smells. It lasted just one year. In 1892, the Plymouth Corporation Tramway Department was formed, with its striking vermilion and white window pillars. The arrival of electricity at the turn of the century certainly revolutionised street transport, and the Devonport and District Tramway Company made full use of this innovation, by forming their electric network in 1901.

Passengers waiting for the Cremyll ferry linking Stonehouse and Plymouth, around 1913. Records for this ferry go back to the eleventh century, and rights of crossing the Tamar at this point even further back into antiquity. Tradition has it that women from Saltash rowed the Black Prince across this passage of water to join his troops. The first owners of the ferry were the Valletorts; later it came into the hands of the Mount Edgcumbe family. It was the main mail route for Cornwall, but its unreliability was renowned, due to the hazardous meeting of three tides. There was no steam boat on the route until 1889. The carrier was the largest of three boats in the early nineteenth century; she made the crossing at a speed of ten knots, and carried a hundred and fifty passengers.

Cremyll, near Devonport

The austere figure of one of Plymouth's most famous sons – Robert Falcon Scott, born in Outlands, Devonport in 1868, the son of a local brewer. His was a life which was to be destroyed by a single-minded obsession: to be the first to reach the South Pole. He was to have this goal snatched away from him by the more mature, better-disciplined and prepared Norwegian, Roald Amundsen. Scott is seen here with his wife Kathleen, a talented scupltress, whom he married in 1908. Kathleen Bruce was the daughter of a Nottinghamshire vicar. She was a vegetarian who abhorred alcohol, and her main desire in life was to have a son. Scott was to fulfill that wish, when Peter Markham Scott was born in 1909. Kathleen was positively bowled over by Scott on her first meeting with him. She particularly noticed his ' … very small waist, a rare smile, and with eyes of a quite unnaturally dark blue, almost purple. I have never seen their like'. After Scott's death, she married Lord Kennett, and she herself died in 1947.

Halfpenny Bridge, Devonport

In 1767, an Act of Parliament was passed for the building of a bridge across Stonehouse Creek from Stonehouse to Plymouth Dock. It was commissioned by George, Lord Edgcumbe and Sir John Aubyn; John Smeaton, who'd just completed his lighthouse off Eddystone Rocks, was the designer. It was opened in 1773, but it wasn't toll-free. For the privilege of using the bridge, you had to pay a halfpenny. Nothing was more calculated to stir up resentment than this charge. People hated it, and one 19th century guide wrote 'it impedes the traffic, is an unnecessary and unjust tax upon pedestrians and carts and carriages, and is of no use to anyone except the lords of the manor, who realise something like £2,000 annually from its receipts.' The halfpenny bridge became the inspiration for a popular ballad:

Lord Edgcumbe, Earl Divine
All the hakey fish are thine
All the fishes off Penlee
Lordy Edgcumbe belong to thee.

Lordy Edgcumbe up the hill
'Tis a shame to treat us ill
Marines and soldiers
       go through free
Yet the sailor has to pay his dee

Lordy Edgcumbe good and great
Open wide the Halfpenny Gate
For your credit and renown
Pull the bloody toll gate down.

The bridge did eventually fall into the hands of the civic authorities, and on April 1 1924, all toll gates at Millbridge, Laira, Embankment and Stonehouse were set free. There must have been some celebrations on that day!

Spectators from Plymouth gather for the best vantage point, at the River Yealm Regatta of 1919. It must have been quite a sight, and a lovely summer day's outing. All were dressed accordingly.

Left, a sailing cargo boat at Steer Point, on the River Yealm. The boat was docked to load bricks from the local brick factory.

And a solitary man on the beach at Wembury Rocks, near the Mewstone, on the mouth of the Yealm, gathers seaweed for fertilizer. His horse waits patiently. The boat in the water looks as if she's seen much better days.

A sturdy bunch of men indeed, and a group one would readily trust at sea in a situation of danger or distress. They're the River Yealm lifeboat crew, and their cork jackets look like some weird sort of musical instruments. They wore leather boots and red tam o'shanter hats. Mr Hockaday, a resident of Noss who lent me this photo, tells me there are five Hockadays in this formidable team.

One of Plymouth's passenger steamers speeding up the River Kitley
and approaching the 'Pool', the name given to the harbour at Noss
Mayo. Also in sight, two house-boats. A more common sight nowadays
is the yacht. There was a great deal of competition for trips up such
rivers, and rivalry amongst boat companies was not always friendly.

Streets ahead! Number 2 is Charlie Axworthy, a local fisherman,
who's well out in the lead on the Revelstone run, a nine-mile
Membland Drive marathon. A pony and trap waits to pick up those
who didn't complete the race. It was a race which continued
annually until just before the Second World War.

Totnes

Below, a busy day in Totnes High Street. The market town got its name from two Saxon words: tot, which means look out and nais, meaning nose. The best relic of its ancient circuit of walls around the city is east Gate, right, in Fore Street and High Street. Totnes was once the richest town in Devon, after Exeter, and was famous for many industries, including quarrying, wool, shipbuilding and tanning.

A COTTAGE in Totnes; an old man and woman pose like statues for Mr Frith the photographer in 1905. Who they are is now long-forgotten, but it comes as no surprise that Frith chose this couple. For what a marvellous study they make of an elderly Victorian pair. It's not difficult to speculate on the sort of life they'd led: probably one of hardship and endurance, of stoicism and self-discipline. But they weathered the storms together and there's a dignity and poise about them which is very compelling.

You can almost smell the bacon and eggs frying in this substantial lady's pan, as she cooks up breakfast for the troops. The date is around 1905, and Hancock's Fair is in Totnes, bringing a touch of gaiety to the town. The steam traction engine, from Bristol, brought the power to drive all the fair organs and rides.

One of the many pleasant pastimes for Victorians was a gentle cruise up the river by paddle steamer. Here a boat waits at the landing stage at Totnes, around 1896, bound for Dartmouth. Although a bright sunny day, note all the dark umbrellas raised to protect fair, delicate ladies' skin.

A group of Kingsbridge townspeople tucks in for a celebration lunch on the Diamond Jubilee of their beloved Queen in 1897. I love this photograph because of its detail and light. You can get close up to the ladies and define the textures of their clothes, their bonnets, and even their dangly earrings. If only it were possible to overhear their conversations …

*This picture, taken outside the White Hart Hotel, Kingsbridge, was on
a fair day around 1890. Before the First World War, a crab smack
came to the town every couple of weeks from Southampton, and the
crabs were kept alive in a well in the bowels of the ship. The ladies
selling them at this long table do not look as if they'd be in the mood
for bargaining; shrewd businesswomen they undoubtedly were!*

Left, Kingsbridge Poor House, which was situated at the top of Union Street. Devon was a county which had seen its fair share of poverty and hardship, and many families throughout the centuries had found it difficult to make ends meet. All poor people were united in their fear and dread of the workhouse, with all the shame and degradation it conjured up. And the larger the institution, the grimmer it usually was. People reduced to vagrancy preferred to roam the countryside, rather than end up in the workhouse. In the early nineteenth century, each village ran its own poor houses, but by the middle of the century, unions were formed by several villages in the Kingsbridge area to centralise all the paupers under one roof. This union workhouse was built in 1837 at a cost of £6,000. It could house around three hundred and fifty, but numbers rarely reached more than eighty five. Conditions were like something out of Dickens. A nurse was employed to look after the inhabitants, but imagine one poor soul tending to the needs of so many, with illnesses like typhoid, scarlet fever and small pox rife. This particular nurse, it's recorded, was dismissed for hitting the gin bottle a bit too hard one day. And who can blame her? Actually though, even the inmates got gin rations each week, but perhaps they'd have preferred to forego such a luxury for better food.

Hallsands

Right – Two views of the tiny village of Hallsands, which experienced at first hand the ravages of storms and sea. Originally the village was built along a narrow, flat rock, standing well above sea level, and protected by a large pebble beach. This was a tailor-made place for fishing, an occupation taken up by virtually all the inhabitants. Crabbing and seine net fishing were very successful money spinners, and when shoals were spotted, high on a cliff the 'hurler' would warn the waiting men, who'd clamber into their boats, casting their nets and encircling the unsuspecting shoals. There were record catches on many occasions, all of which were taken to London for sale, via the nearest town of Kingsbridge. Sometimes the catches of pilchards were so large that the fish were processed into fertilizer.

Here, a group of hardened and weather-beaten locals take time out for the photographer, as they go about the vital job of making crab pots. These were made from withies, grown in the nearby marshes, and many farms cultivated withy groves. At the first new moon of the new year, they'd cut the previous year's growth at the stumps and prepare shoots for the crab pots.

And so life continued for the people of Hallsands, until the world started to turn sour. When gravel was needed for the extension of the naval dockyard at Devonport in Plymouth, eyes turned to Start Bay, and from 1897, dredging began to affect the daily lives of the fishermen. True, they did receive some compensation, but not until 650,000 tons of sand, gravel and shingle had been dragged from the sea bed. The ensuing storms of 1903, 1904 and 1917 were unarguable proof that the high pebble ridge on which the village depended had been severely undermined by such dredging. Many homes, dwellings and livelihoods were swept away by the sea.

For many years, the only person living in the village was an old woman called Elizabeth Prettyjohn. Her home, a run-down shack, was shared with her goats and chickens. But she refused to move, and died there in the 1960s.

Making merry at Salcombe. A relaxed party of picnickers enjoys lunch on the beach, shoes kicked off, petticoats hitched up and beer glasses at the ready. It's unusual to see such gay abandon, and the group may well have been on holiday, so felt absolutely entitled to let their hair down – once they'd removed their straw boaters! They obviously enjoyed music too – note the gramophone on the left and the string instrument being strummed on the right.

The fishwives of Beesands in 1898. The two younger women haven't yet been as ravaged by wind and work as their older sisters, but they too would have had a life of hardship and struggling to look forward to. There must, however, have been a tremendous companionship amongst them, a banding together and a willingness to help each other that many small village communities still manage to maintain.

Fisherwomen and their young sons, pulling in the seine nets around 1896. With their distinctive white head-dresses they cut a sturdy figure on the beaches of Hallsands, Start Bay and East Portlemouth, and proved themselves an invaluable help to the men.

Dartmouth

DARTMOUTH – the name to stir noble emotions in the hearts and minds of sailors for centuries. For tiny fishing boats to the big steamers of the nineteenth century the deep waters of the harbour have been a haven; the Britannia Naval College was, and is still, THE place for all would-be naval officers to attend.

Although the Naval Academy at Portsmouth trained many officers before 1837, it wasn't until 1827 that a regular system of training cadets in a special centre, then sending them on to a man-of-war, was established. HMS Britannia was moved up the harbour of the River Dart as a training ship for naval cadets in 1868. She was anchored above a floating bridge, and later joined by HMS Hindostan, who lay alongside her. Britannia was a three-decker, with roomy gun decks for sleeping, training and instruction. The news of this move to Dartmouth was not welcomed by places such as Weymouth, Plymouth and Portsmouth. This was a great prize they'd lost in terms of both commerce and prestige, and voices were raised in Parliament at the wisdom of such a choice.

However, the Royal seal of approval was given by the Prince of Wales in 1877, who went on to send two of his sons to the training ship. The permanence of the base was confirmed in 1896, when the Admiralty purchased the old manor house of Mount Boone from the Seale family.

Young cadets began their training at the tender age of fifteen, and they received instruction in seamanship and navigation. No general education was yet on offer. They remained there for three years, before they were sent off to join the fleet. A rather limited beginning to a career which could well lead on to commanding ships in battles like Jutland. But after 1902, when the foundation stone for the college was laid by Edward VII, it was decided the young men needed a wider education, and one certainly as good as any public school could offer. So training was extended to four years, and a proper civilian staff was employed to teach them.

A good view of the very early beginnings of HMS Britannia Royal Naval College, with HMS Britannia, a veteran of Trafalgar, on the right.

The year is 1898, and King George and Queen Mary are in Dartmouth, with their smartly-dressed entourage, complete with Jack Russell dog in the background. Dartmouth was no stranger to royal visits; William II sailed from here for Normandy, Richard I left here for the Crusades in 1190, and Charles II is said to have spent a night at a house in the Butterwalk. Later came Edward VII, George V, and his two sons Prince George and Prince Edward. And right, the mayor of Dartmouth welcomes two new, rather special recruits: Prince George and Prince Edward, in 1911.

1905 and a nostalgic moment for so many, as the old Hindostan, which came to Dartmouth in 1864, and was moored alongside the first HMS Britannia, makes her way out of harbour, to be broken up for scrap.

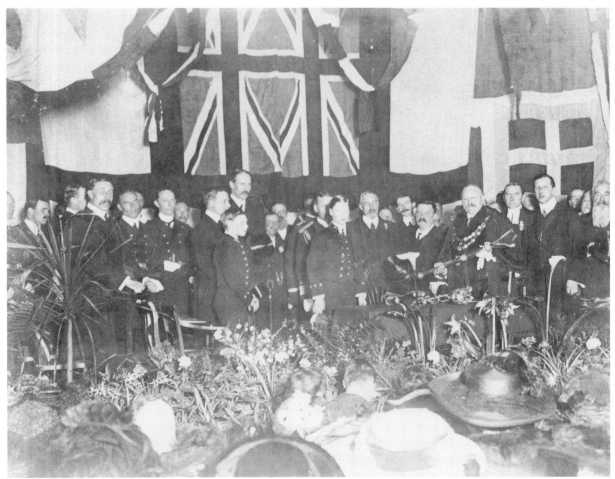

The second HMS Britannia, formerly the Prince of Wales, around 1869. The townspeople certainly must have welcomed an influx of over 250 cadets into their town, and made sure that all their needs were well catered for. Many a tidy living must have been made from them.

The Royal Avenue Gardens, Dartmouth, with the original bandstand in the background. Many sea-faring yarns must have been exchanged here amongst the old sailors, who sauntered out into the sunshine from their place of refuge, the Sailors' Home. They must have enjoyed the bustle of such a busy working port, constantly expanding with the arrival of the Torbay railway at Kingswear, and the building of quays and jetties to encourage steamer traffic. Dartmouth became the perfect refuelling stop, with its deep, safe harbour.

Brixham

THE LITTLE fishing port of Brixham was called the mother of deep sea fisheries. Permission to trawl on her seabed was granted by an act of Parliament in the 17th century, and from then on Brixham never looked back. As the centuries rolled on, the trawl beams grew bigger, and so did the boats, which were able to fish as far away as the North Sea. The little port ended up virtually colonising Hull and Grimsby.

But it wasn't long before these two ports began to catch on to Brixham's game, and when one day a boat dropped its trawl in the Silver Pits, an area of the North Sea, and the nets came up heaving with Dover soles, Brixham knew its days of holding the monopoly were over. So Brixham men moved on, to the east coast, to the Bristol Channel and the Irish Sea. Their catch was plentiful and varied: ray, sole, plaice, dab, cod and ling. All the men were on a share basis, and when the catch was sold, they all got a share, eight in all. Boys were paid two shillings and sixpence a week, and were entitled to take home hen crabs.

In this postcard, dated 1868, we can see the trawlers with their massive old boomer sails. These were very difficult to handle, and later gave way to ketches, which were much more manoeuvrable.

21556F.   Brixham Trawlers waiting for a Breeze in 1868.

*Boats getting ready for Brixham's annual Regatta. In clear view is the
BM161 Valerian, winner of the King's Cup, presented by George V.
The King was a very keen yachtsman, and his own boats used to sail
in the regatta. Here bottoms of boats are being scrubbed and refits are
being carried out – all with a great sense of occasion and pride.*

Brixham harbour, with the famous statue of William III. We know the postcard is after 1889, because this statue was built at that date and put on the beach out in the harbour. In 1898 the harbour was re-built and the statue was included in the new harbour. The Furneaux shipyard used to stand on the left.

Boats were all built out in the open, and two boatyards – J.W. and A. Oppen, and Dewdney worked side by side. Brixham boats were renowned, and hundreds of British sailors have Brixham to thank for their vessels' seaworthiness.

A good view of family life on the beach at Teignmouth. A little girl stares wistfully out to sea as she holds on to her doll's pram. In the background, the town's pier constructed in the 1880s, at a cost of £8,000. Its original owners were the Devon Dock Pier and Steamship Company. It was 600 ft long, with seats all the way up for 'promenaders' and 'loungers'. The buildings at the seaward end were completed ten years later. The pier had its critics at the time; people complained that it cut the view of the full length of the foreshore in two. Teignmouth became independent from Exeter as a port in its own right in 1852.

Below, teatime at the riverside gardens in Teignmouth. Aspidistras adorn the tables, the ladies look splendid in their wide-brimmed hats, and gentlemen sport jackets and straw boaters. All is elegance and civility – the perfect end to a day's outing. On the menu – local damson and strawberry jams to spread on home-made scones, with a generous bowl of thick, yellow clotted cream to top it off. For those a little more peckish, a full lobster tea could be had for just 2s 6d. Cockle teas were also a speciality.

This extraordinary pair of whale's jawbones, right, was once a famous landmark in Teignmouth, and was erected at the end of the pier by Mr Pike Ward, whose family were involved with the Newfoundland trade. The bones were eventually removed by the town council, and unceremoniously dumped on the tip, which did not go down well, as local papers of the time testify.

Jaw Bones, Teignmouth.

Tea Gardens, "Coombe Cellars", on the River Teign, Teignmouth. Part of Tea Terrace.

T. Harding, Son & Co. (Bristol.) 02045.P. Real Photo Series

These little mites look so appealing, as they stand in the street at Dawlish, collecting money for horses wounded in the First World War. The donkey, a sad specimen himself, is called Fred. Further research into the picture reveals the people are, left to right, Herbert Thorp, Joan Webbing and Harry Mitchell. Who but the hardest hearted could have resisted giving these children a few pennies?

Boating Cove, Dawlish.   *N 1900.*

Two children dig for treasure in the sand at Boating Cove, Dawlish. It must have been a good summer in 1900; the sender of the postcard, a lady called Nellie, remarks 'what lovely weather we're having!' The town of Dawlish developed as a fashionable resort and retirement haven during the 19th century. Sea bathing became 'de rigeur', but the town's authorities thought fit to warn visitors of certain precautions they should take, as seen in the ''Hints to Bathers'', in Dawlish's Pavilion – *'some sea water may be thrown over the head when first entering the sea, so as to equalise the temperature of the body, to avoid propelling the blood to the head too swiftly . . . even strong persons much accustomed to bathing are liable to be depressed by a bath taken before breakfast'.*

Ilfracombe

ILFRACOMBE had considerable importance in the fourteenth century, and Edward III asked the town to provide six vessels and one hundred men for his invasion of France. Liverpool, a much bigger port, could only raise one vessel and five men! Its ship-building industry was almost legendary, its harbour a decent size, and its trade excellent, in fish, metals, wool, wine and leather to name but a few.

The rapid growth of such trade meant almost inevitably a more than passing interest in the age-old custom of smuggling. Everybody seemed to have some stake in it, and it was said the townspeople could be divided into two classes – smugglers and customs officers. At the beginning of the nineteenth century, there were fifteen hundred rates of customs duty. Some bureaucracy! But the Crown found it almost impossible to nail convictions on those suspected of smuggling, so an amnesty was offered to those smugglers who would turn customs officers.

But for those who persisted in the trade, the pickings were rich, and the wilds of Exmoor were the perfect hiding places for their loot.

A day of pomp and circumstance for the townspeople of Ilfracombe as they come out into the streets to celebrate the Diamond Jubilee of their beloved Queen Victoria. It must have been a familiar scene in hundreds of towns and cities all over the kingdom. This procession – June 22 1897 – has just reached Wilder Street, so-called because of the stream which ran close by. The town's brass band provides music for the occasion, while local dignitaries take to their horse-drawn carriages.

Weddings are usually happy occasions, especially once the service is over and guests look forward to the reception. Whether this wedding party, captured at Ilfracombe around 1900 is feeling a bit put out at having to squash together in the back yard with only a piece of old carpet to stand on, is difficult to fathom. And so are most of the group's expressions. The bride's family look less than ecstatic, especially the seated lady in the black beaded cape. Decidedly tight lipped! At least the groom looks moderately hopeful that it will all come out in the wash.

The seasonal donkey rides around Ilfracombe and the surrounding countryside were always a popular day out for tourists and locals alike, and one of the departure points was at the back of the Runnycleve Hotel. Perhaps this was a special occasion, this ninth day of September 1896, because everybody, but everybody, wants to get into the picture. Net curtains are pulled back, staff hang out of the windows and the crowd stands to attention. The buxom white-aproned ladies have settled their charges into their donkey-drawn carriages ready for the off. These sturdy creatures had a long hike ahead; the favourite trip was the Tors walk, the seven hills above the town, facing the Bristol Channel, known locally as the Severn Sea.

The first mobile chip shop for the town of Ilfracombe, courtesy of the Norman family of 2 Ivy Cottages. The mouth-watering smell of hot potatoes must have wafted through the town on many a cold winter's night, and customers were never in short supply. The spuds were chipped as required by operating a lever on the right hand side, and the machine, which was coal-fired, cooked them in rich beef dripping. The little boy in his white apron is now a grown man, and father of Raymond Norman of Ilfracombe. In overalls is his grandfather, Frederick Norman, and the other two are town road sweeper John Norman and Runnycleve Hotel porter George Norman. A name to be reckoned with in the town!

A great day of celebration for the North Devon town of Lynton, with the final opening of their long-awaited railway on September 17, 1895. The procession is on its way to Castle Hill and Lynbridge, escorted by two bands, the Royal North Devon Hussars and the Lynton Season Band. As the day was declared a public holiday, the numbers swelled as people from the twin towns of Lynton and Lynmouth joined the railway directors, the Mayor, the lifeboat crew, coastguards and hundreds of school children.
Lady Newnes, wife of Sir George Newnes, who was one of the biggest patrons of the scheme, cut the first sod of the new line, using a silver spade. Afterwards, invited guests retired to the Valley of the Rocks Hotel for a slap-up lunch. Plans for the railway showed that the cost would not exceed £2,500 a mile, and the length would be 1,916 miles in all. It meant the journey from Lynton to Barnstaple would take just one hour.

Above, *a comfortable middle-class home in Lynton and a carefully-posed photograph for the family album. Mother reads a doubtless improving book, father holds small child in laced boots who would probably rather be exploring the summertime garden. Windows stand open to the sunshine.*

Below, *Mars Hill at Lynmouth. The driver of the horse and cart on the left could be making his way to the pub on the right. Its signboard, reading the Rising Sun, is almost hidden amongst the lush climbing plants, but no doubt the thirsty labourer knows where to find the door. Note the two differing street lights.*

Lynmouth was just a cluster of fishermen's cottages before the wealthy, kept at home by the Napoleonic wars, began to look at the more remote parts of Devon and Cornwall as potential holiday resorts. Attracted by its wild beauty, early tourists began visiting the area and inns and tearooms opened up to cater for them. Scenes such as this below, with falls sparkling in the sun, cascading below a rustic bridge, stirred Victorian writers to pen pastoral poetry and artists to set up their easels in such delightful spots.

TWO OUTSTANDING natural beauty spots that North Devon is rightly proud of: Watersmeet at Lynmouth and the Valley of the Rocks at Lynton. Watersmeet is so-called because of the junction of the East Lyn and Coombe Park water. It really is an uplifting place to visit, whatever your mood, with its gushing cascades, rustic bridges, and stunning bird life. The Valley of the Rocks reveals a sterner aspect of nature, a more rugged and barren beauty. Legend has it that Lynton Castle stood just near the Valley, and a Black Monk took a dislike to the owner of this castle, putting a curse upon him. All this man's family were told that they'd be under the monk's spell until they saw a lady's child, beckoning them into the porch of the Holy Church. When the man's son did eventually see this strange sight, the Black Monk threw himself into the abyss below. To make the story really dramatic, and round it off nicely, it's then rumoured that there was a huge earthquake, with the castle vanishing and the huge rocks we see today being thrown up in its place. The Cheesewring on the left is mentioned in R.D. Blackmore's Lorna Doone, and is the spot where Jan Ridd came to seek Mother Meldrum's advice on his love life.

Clovelly

Clovelly – the ultimate in tourist experience, a perfect unspoilt, quaint part of Devon, with its cobbled streets tumbling down for half a mile to the sea, the cottages bedecked with flowers and their windows thrown open to strong salty smells. There was, and is, no place for the motor car here; the donkey rules supreme. The village's layout dates from the 1660s, but as fire destroyed practically all records, it's hard to know what it was like before this date. We do know that a stream of water used to run down the right side of the streets, with tiny bridges crossing to the cottages. It was this water that Charles Kingsley, who had lived there when his father was rector, blamed for the out-break of cholera of 1861. And it was he who pushed for the water to be covered up. Kingsley must have got much of his inspiration for *Westward Ho!* from Clovelly, which he described as this 'dear old paradise'.

An Edwardian photographer frames the High Street at Clovelly. The struggling donkey pauses before continuing his steep, slow climb up the slope, while the lady painter remains absorbed with her brush strokes. Little has changed in almost a century, and artists still flock to capture scenes identical to this one. A comforting thought: Clovelly remains unspoilt, and its natural beauty is untarnished and unchanging.

A boy makes his way up the slope at Clovelly. He used this sledge for transporting goods up and down the steep road that runs through the village. It must have been quite a grind for children so young to have to grow up so quickly. There was precious little time for such youngsters to enjoy themselves, or have the luxury of moments 'to stand and stare.'

Two ketches beached up in Combemartin harbour around 1890. The boat on the right, the 35-ton Sir T.D. Acland, was built at Bude in 1861. Both vessels were owned by Mr George Irwin of Combemartin. Here, coal is being loaded onto a waiting horse-drawn cart. Combemartin was anciently known as Marhuscombe. Silver and lead mines were established here in the reign of Edward I, when 330 men were brought from the Derbyshire Peaks to work them. And in Edward III's reign, the produce from these mines helped to defray the expenses of his war with France.

Hangman Hills, Combe Martin, a grim name conjuring up thoughts of gallows and highwaymen. But the name derives from the Celtic for boundary stone and the heather-clad moorland, much of it now owned by the National Trust, is a peaceful place to walk and look down on the calm waters below. Combe Martin itself made history centuries ago when its rich mines gave up their silver to help pay for the Hundred Years War.

You could hardly find a more typical rectory than Georgeham, its elegant facade, with white-painted shutters, redolent of respectability and rectitude. The staff, lined up outside, take their duties seriously and pose solemn-faced for the camera. A retriever slumbers at the feet of his master. Behind them, sash windows are open with mathematical precision at exactly the same height for the morning sweeping and dusting.

The beautiful, almost cathedral-like, interior of St Helen's Church on Lundy. The church, built of local stone, took a year to build and was completed and dedicated in 1897. There is also an ancient ruined chapel dedicated to St Helen traditionally held to have been in use, at least for funerals, since the reign of William and Mary. The modern church has a statue of its patron saint above the entrance. The island of Lundy has belonged to the National Trust since 1969.

Access to Lundy is difficult. Nowadays there is a track from the landing beach useable by a tractor but here, the old horse-drawn landing stage, mounted on cartwheels, is being put in place. This was probably not for tourists, a modern addition to life on the windswept island, but to land vital supplies for the farming which brought its residents a precarious living. Not all activities on the island were so blameless. Lundy was a favourite sheltering place for pirates and a popular haunt for smugglers in more lawless times.

The village of Lundy and its main street looking bleak and barren in this picture taken from the top of the church tower in the 1920s. Manor Farm, the large building in the foreground, was then a hotel. Lundy remains a Mecca for tourists, many interested in the abundant wildlife. Lundy boasts the first marine reserve in the country with its colonies of seals, its seabirds, and ashore the wild goats and deer proving endlessly fascinating to holidaymakers and naturalists alike.

Bideford

The last widening of Bideford Quay in progress – from 1889 to 1890. This was just one of many improvements the town was enjoying at the time. With the arrival of the railway in 1855, the tourists came flocking in to visit the famous sea port – the port which gave five ships for the Spanish Armada, the home town of Sir Richard Grenville and Charles Kingsley, whose marble figure still stands by the River Torridge. And a flourishing town needed all modern amenities. The town was completely re-sewered in 1871, the railway was extended to Torrington in 1872 and the first purpose-built hospital opened in 1876. All this provided much-needed work for the townspeople, and in 1894, a Bideford guide book proudly stated 'No town in the west of England has grown so rapidly, and few have been so radically improved'.

Barnstaple

The Royal Fortescue Hotel, in Barnstaple's Boutport Street. It was
considered to be one of the best establishments in the town, and it was
from here that the Royal Mail coach left every morning at six o'clock
sharp. The return of the London coach became a very important event
in Barnstaple, attracting large crowds eager for news of the Big City.
For those unfortunates who had to make the trip to London by such a
coach, they could reckon on a journey of fifty-odd hours, costing £3.
Perhaps not renowned as a beauty spot, Barnstaple still has its
charms, and it was described by a 19th century poet thus: 'thou art
more fair than people deem, bright town beside Taw's winding
stream'. Samuel Pepys's wife was a Barnstaple girl, and the poet Gay
is also supposed to have been born there.

Barnstaple claims to be the oldest borough in England and as befits its status has this magnificent Square, with a clock-tower in memory of Prince Albert. This picture was taken on a sunny summer afternoon and the photographer standing behind his tripod must have been annoyed to have the serenity of the scene spoilt by the inquisitive dog on the right. But apart from the dog, Barnstaple slumbered on. The guests at Toll's Private Hotel in the centre were probably having afternoon tea. What a contrast to the scene today with the Square thronged with cars.

Barnstaple Fair, circa 1910, and what a magnificent collection of human beings, faces all staring into the camera, pressing forward to be part of the photograph. It's a great opportunity to examine those faces close up, and a photo I never tire of looking at. It's interesting to note that almost all of the men over thirty sport either a moustache or a beard, and there's just one bare head – a lad who may be in trouble when he gets home for losing his cap.

A rare old photograph of Barnstaple showing the lake and Cypress Island. The lake was filled in in 1897.

RESIDENTS of Appledore, taking a closer look at boats moored at the town's quay. On the left, the ketch Happy Return, and on the right, the topsail schooner Countess Caithness. The town earned itself a high reputation in the boat-building world, and at the Great Exhibition of 1851 the Duke of Northumberland, who was President of the RNLI, offered a hundred guineas for the best model of a lifeboat. There were 280 entries, and second prize went to an unknown Appledore boatbuilder by the name of Henry Hinks. He designed a boat which could carry 40 men at a cost of £110. And in 1924, an associate of Mr Hink's firm broke up one of the last of England's old 'wooden walls', the Revenge, of Battle of Trafalgar fame. The first paddle steamer, the Torridge, sailed up the river to Bideford from Appledore in 1835.

MORE BOSSINEY BOOKS ...

E.V. THOMPSON'S WESTCOUNTRY
This is a memorable journey: a combination of colour and black-and-white photography.
'Stunning photographs and fascinating facts make this an ideal book for South West tourists and residents alike – beautifully atmospheric colour shots make browsing through the pages a real delight.'
Jane Leigh, Express & Echo

MYSTERIOUS PLACES
by Peter Underwood
Visits locations that 'seem to have been touched by a magic hand'. The man who has been called Britain's No. 1 ghost hunter reflects: 'We live in a very mysterious world .'
'. . . an insight into some of the more mysterious places in the south west.'
David Elvidge
Launceston & Bude Gazette

COASTLINE OF CORNWALL
by Ken Duxbury
Ken Duxbury has spent thirty years sailing the seas of Cornwall, walking its clifftops, exploring its caves and beaches, using its harbours and creeks.
'. . . a trip in words and pictures from Hawker's Morwenstow in the north, round Land's End and the Lizard to the gentle slopes of Mount Edgcumbe country park.'
The Western Morning News

MYSTERIES IN THE DEVON LANDSCAPE
by Hilary Wreford & Michael Williams
Outstanding photographs and illuminating text about eerie aspects of Devon. Seen on TSW and Channel 4. Author interviews on Devon Air and BBC Radio Devon.
'. . . reveals that Devon has more than its share of legends and deep folklore.'
Derek Henderson
North Devon Journal Herald

CASTLES OF DEVON
by James Mildren
The well-known Westcountry journalist tours 16 castles.
'Mr Mildren, whose love for the Westcountry is obvious and contagious, digs out many fascinating nuggets . . .'
Western Evening Herald

DART – THE MAGICAL RIVER
by Ken Duxbury
Rising high on Dartmoor, the twin rivers, East and West Dart, merge to flow to the sea at Dartmouth.
'The book is a clever blend of history, topography and personalities, all of which combine to create a marvellous image of both the river and its communities.'
Richard Armstrong, Totnes Times

PLYMOUTH IN WAR & PEACE
by Guy Fleming
Bossiney's 150th title by the well-known journalist of the Western Evening Herald. Never has the saying 'every picture tells a story' been more vividly demonstrated. The blitz and Plymouth Argyle, famous politicians and the Navy, the Barbican and the rebirth of the city are only some of the features.

HISTORIC INNS OF DEVON
by Monica Wyatt
The author visits 50 famous hostelries scattered over the county.
'Monica Wyatt's writing is pitched at just the right level . . . thoroughly researched, shot through with real enthusiasm and never donnish. She shares her discoveries with you . . . I raise my glass.'
The Western Evening Herald

LEGENDS OF DEVON
by Sally Jones
Devon is a mine of folklore and myth. Here is a journey through legendary Devon. Sally Jones brings in to focus some fascinating tales, showing us that the line dividing fact and legend is an intriguing one.
'Sally Jones had trodden the path of legendary Devon well . . .'
Tavistock Times

WESTCOUNTRY MYSTERIES
Introduced by Colin Wilson
A team of authors probe mysterious happenings in Somerset, Devon and Cornwall. Drawings and photographs all add to the mysterious content.
'A team of authors have joined forces to re-examine and prove various yarns from the puzzling to the tragic.'
James Belsey, Bristol Evening Post

MY CORNWALL
A personal vision of this Celtic land by eleven writers: Daphne du Maurier, Ronald Duncan, James Turner, Angela du Maurier, Jack Clemo, Denys Val Baker, Colin Wilson, C.C. Vyvyan, Arthur Caddick, Michael Williams and Derek Tangye with reproductions of paintings by Margo Maeckelberghe and splendid black and white photographs.
'. . . gives a valuable insight into the many facets of this fascinating land . . .'
John Marquis, The Falmouth Packet

MORE BOSSINEY BOOKS ...

AGATHA CHRISTIE'S DEVON
Jane Langton

CURIOSITIES OF EXMOOR
Felicity Young

DEVON MYSTERIES
Judy Chard

ABOUT EXMOOR
Polly Lloyd

UNKNOWN DEVON
Rosemary Anne Lauder, Michael Williams and Monica
Wyatt

GHOSTS OF DEVON
Peter Underwood

LOCATION – CORNWALL
David Clarke

STRANGE STORIES FROM DEVON
Rosemary Anne Lauder and Michael Williams

SUPERNATURAL IN CORNWALL
Michael Williams

We shall be pleased to send you our catalogue giving full details of our growing list of titles for Devon, Cornwall, Dorset, Somerset and Wiltshire as well as forthcoming publications. If you have difficulty in obtaining our titles write direct to Bossiney Books, Land's End, St Teath, Bodmin, Cornwall